EXISTENCE

A Collection of Poetry

Moon Johnson

Dedication:

Dear Mom,

I wouldn't be on earth if it weren't for your existence and I wouldn't have made it past 16 years old if it weren't for your Love. Thank you for giving me life, thank you for saving my life, and thank you for being such an amazing role model. "Existence" couldn't be possible without you so with this dedication I celebrate you as both my mother and my hero.

All my Love, Moon.

p.s. HAPPY BIRTHDAY !

PROLOGUE

"Poetry; bits of existence broken into language,
an abstract form of self portrait."

- Moon Johnson

what more does
LOVE
ask of us
other than to be
expressed?

i saw an eternity
in his eyes and
suddenly
i was overwhelmed with
the urge
to slit his throat.
    i'd miss him too much
    i kissed him instead,
took a bite out
of the risk,
      swallowed.

kissing his skin
feels like an act of
rebellion
      blackness normality

                  i entangle myself
                  within his kinks
                  not as a revolutionary
                        statement,
      but because i lay my head here.

          his soul is the home
          my ancestors
entrusted to me.

violate my space
    my face
like the steam from
a cup of tea

    consume me
perfume me
    in the scent of your affection

the soul's orgasms last longer..
    appeal to her first

love me like

    a tree.

       wind,

         rain,

      snow,

    sleet,

          stay.

everything
makes sense
in her presence.

     silence
   becomes poetry
in the space she occupies.

        her face is
     the shape of a
          future
     i can't
       un-want.

my laughter often
speckled
across her chest
freckled flesh
she wore my joy
on her skin
        so soft
my lips
        so close
            so gently
    kissing her collarbone
burying my face
                into her neck
                into the smell
        of sage,
coconuts,
and the rest of
        our little eternity
    if forever
had a scent

the mysteries of our world
intrigue me
just as much as
all the rooms of your
mind

i'd invite you into
mine
but you're already
occupying space there.

i hide my fascination
behind a smile
we both pretend
is platonic.

i think
i love
you

you feel particularly infinite.

the point is to
find a
love
who doesn't suffocate
you
and to
drown in them.

a
love
that will burn
your demons
only to birth
angels
from
ashes.

a
love
true enough
to sail to
forever
on.

he doesn't pet me like a zoo animal,
his admiration isn't soaking with ignorance,
and i'm not a circus freak when i go a week
without washing my hair.

he caresses these tendrils,
takes naps in these naps,
remembers to tie my bonnet a little tighter
before back shots,
black shots,
his kisses taste of Hennessy
translated to honey on my lips.
My hips sway
to the rhythm of his understanding.
He doesn't just look at me,
he sees me
with generations of shared pride,
struggle,
and culture
dripping from his gaze.

our love is power,
a black love as strong as our roots
pouring out of our pores like liquid gold,
puddling at our ankles
like the broken chains of our ancestors.

we dance in each other
unapologetically
splattering the roads we walk
in shades of freedom and
hues of excellence.

patience escapes me

faces,
names,
intentions change
as the seasons do

affections crave
intimacy,
feigns consistency,
both lack substance
when you leave before dawn

i've learned to clean my sheets
and tread depth
with light feet
so i may run
before i am ran from,
never giving myself the chance
to fall.

from whom did i learn
to allow others to take from me
more than they have the ability
to give?

from whom did i learn
to find comfort
in discomfort?

from whom
can i learn
the opposite?

it's
not enough
for you
to like me back.

you have to
act like
it.

15

faulty lover,
please clarify
how many burn marks
to the flesh
one must endure for you

when will your affection
resemble
water

instead of flame.

passion defined by pain.

faulty lover,
please clarify
how you could
ever call this
love?

i grew more and more silent.
my thoughts eating me alive
as if i'm not the only one
whom can hear them.

they scream and they scream
louder and louder begging
for a response they'll never get.

as he sinks his teeth into me
as far as they can go

        i feel nothing.

    as the blood
    slithers across my flesh surface
      staining the underbelly
of my will a deep red,

    i feel nothing.

his moans of pleasure
disgust me
as i allow yet another succubus
to drain me
of whatever essence
i have left.

   i feel absolutely nothing.

    i am
but
   a vacant shell,
      numb,
    waiting by the window
  desperately
     longing
       for my
         return home.

elsewhere

barefoot in the grass.
face toward the sun,
book in one hand,
heart exposed in the other,

escaping,
escaping from
reality, reality,
a reality i no longer identify with

sometimes
   i wake up

      and forget
       that

           i am art.

worn,
comfortable,
my favorite pair of shoes.
dirty, sentimental, familiar,
something i'd like to keep forever
something destined to be replaced.

a fickle kind of significant,
a presence of fleeting importance,
an importance of fleeting presence

the weight of your temporary rests on my chest,
anchoring me to a choice
i'm not courageous enough to make.
i love you but
my heels bleed.
the pain
sole-less
glass adorned toes
graveled ankles.

she
    folds
        in

    on

herself,

    disappearing into

    the pain.

        here all monsters

        look the same.

a shell of who
you
once were
provides opportunity
to fill yourself up
with who
you
want to be.

black
isn't the
darkest
darkness

i wish
there were a color
to describe the current

    gape in my   existence.

i come to you
 bare,
      nude from
         the soul down.

you lash out
as if

it's too much trouble
to listen
            too much trouble
       to love me.

if the wind
were to whisk me away
would my problems finally

feel as nonexistent
as i do?

you're the dreamy texture
she wants to wrap herself in
on rainy days
after the storm neglects
to return her calls
or text back
or show up,

you're the blanket
she always reaches for

her favorite.

soft,
comfortable,
reliable,

utterly unexciting.

suffering in silence
isn't really silent at all

its the loudest pain

you'll ever endure.

i rose from the ashes
a stranger
but i rose.

those who operate in limits
build cages around themselves.

steer clear of those people.

don't get trapped behind bars
that weren't built for you.

when your
dreams
keep you awake at night,

keep
going.

there is
more
to
do.

try

try

try

not to reduce yourself
to flesh.

           it's an assault
               on the soul.

you are survivor
          not victim.

you've won wars.

your healing is your own
and may all who stand in your way
drown in your crimson.

sometimes happiness escapes me.
it drifts away with the tide
leaving a numbness,
a darkness,
a sadness in its wake.

my aches simmer in the sand
for as long as they need
and fade away with the wind

but ignored feelings
are too heavy to float

the only way through them
is through them

let your dreams
        lead the way

they've been there already

we tend to color ourselves
in shades of everyone else's expectations,
then look into the mirror and wonder
why we don't like what we see.

low self-esteem is expensive.
regain control of your expenses.
losing yourself is too big a fee.

some nights
i fall asleep as the moon
and wake up scattered,
            without cohesion.
but
    a starry night,

        though   fragmented,

                    is still

                        something
                to
            marvel
        at.

she built many tunnels behind her ribs,
deep enough where no one could find them.

she stored her wonder there,
in a world exactly opposite
the one she knew.

one need not be naked
to be vulnerable

      knives cut through clothing

      bullets pass through glass

flowers bloom
in silence
and die
just as quiet

trust in
your transformation.

listen to the pleas of
your bones as they
change shape.

introduce yourself to
them again,
and again.

bathe in their pain,
in their wisdom.

find refuge in how temporary
everything is.

i'm starting to realize
the little bit of lonely residing within me
won't stop widening her own void
until i stop settling for a love
less than what i know i deserve

earn my tongue.
i speak from my core
and only ingest conversation
dense in nutrients.

if you cannot feed me,
        relieve me.

i am too much
of a force
for my name
to be spoken in monotone
and for the kisses
placed on my skin
to be few and far
between

either drench me
in love
or soak up the puddle
you claimed was an ocean
and moisten someone else.

i am more.

i require more.

just because
i am strong
doesn't mean you have
to test me

love me ferociously
delicately,

i am precious.

either walk into her with well intention
or walk the fuck away.

i set myself on fire often
i enjoy swimming in the flames
burning all that i was
to fall in love
again
and
again
with all that
i am.

boredom,
not in silence or empty spaces, but
in stagnation, stillness
welcomes overstayed.

creativity suffocates
in sameness, safety,
predictability.

i don't want to know what's next,
i want to create what's next.

i don't want to be safe.
i want to be
free.

i flee
to ocean's edges
and am
instantly reminded
of my limits

and how
i have none.

i disappear from the world
to reappear to myself.
i dance in the wind
prance on leaves
sit blissfully underneath trees,
converse with them,
breathe.

i take naps
on beds of flowers
and dive head first
into stormy seas
run sprints in the earth
sun kissed,
naked,
bushy haired,
happy,
feral,
untamed,
free..

i am
a wild woman.

it's an artist's genetic makeup
to romanticize everything,

a coping mechanism
both gift and curse,
equally as beautiful

as it is dangerous.

some women require more

more conversation
more orgasms
more peace

she doesn't want you
to be her happiness
she wants you
to add to it

if you can't do that

you aren't the more
she's looking for.

the moon
only shines as brightly
as the sun allows her too.
i am both.
i am my own source of light.

what is art

if
not
the
shape

of my existence?

EPILOGUE

"Cleanliness should be reserved for the spirit.
Everything else, filthy, soaking with story."

- Moon Johnson

PRAISE FOR AUTHOR

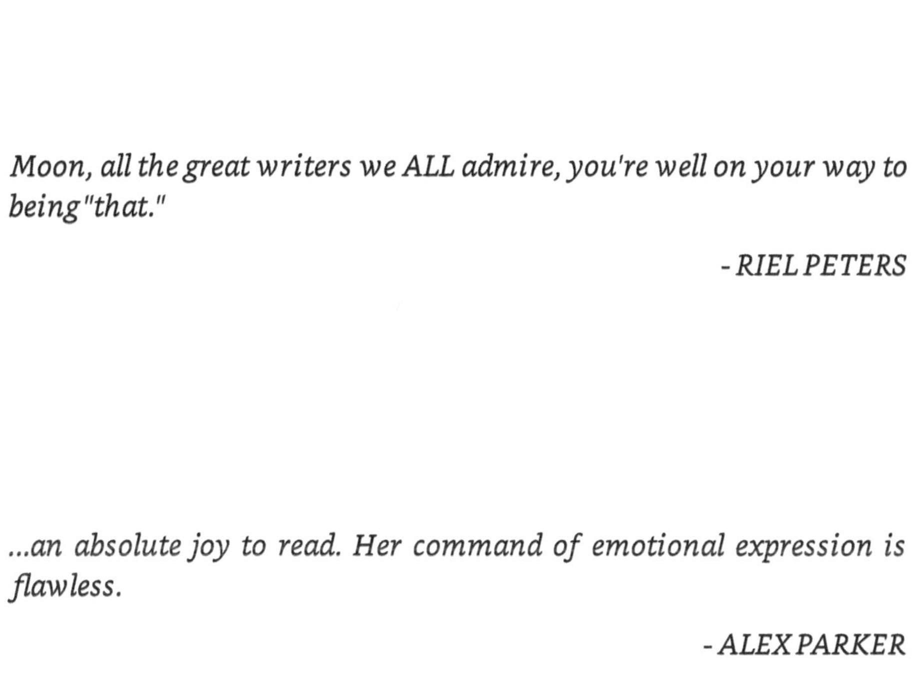

Moon, all the great writers we ALL admire, you're well on your way to being "that."

- RIEL PETERS

...an absolute joy to read. Her command of emotional expression is flawless.

- ALEX PARKER

ABOUT THE AUTHOR

Moon Johnson

Storyteller, filmmaker, poet, muse raised in the San Fernando Valley hills of California rarely felt she had a voice unless there was a pen in her hand. Her life has been far from easy, but she expresses, through her work, how writing has saved her. Two of her poems have been made into short films, one of which has been translated to French. Her words and voice have been featured in mulitple songs streaming worldwide on all music streaming platforms, and her free spirit continues to muse artists and poets, of all mediums, who use her portraits as inspiration for their own creations. Moon finds beauty in even the ugliness of life and has dedicated her existence to telling the truth in such a way she hopes will inspire others to do the same.